P9-CEB-134

What   now?

Ann Patchett

What

HARPER

An Imprint of HarperCollins*Publishers*
www.harpercollins.com

now?

Designed by Chip Kidd

to Allan Gurganus and Alice Stone Ilchman:

What

now?

If all fairy tales begin "Once upon a time," then all graduation speeches begin "When I was sitting where you are now." We may not always say it, at least not in those exact words, but it's what graduation speakers are thinking. We look out at the sea of you and think, Isn't there some mistake? I should still be sitting there. I was that young fifteen minutes ago, I was that beautiful and lost. For me this feeling is compounded by the fact that Sarah Lawrence was my own alma mater. I look out at all these chairs lined up across Westlands lawn and I think, I slept on that lawn, I breathed that wisteria. I batted away those very same bees, or at least I batted away their progenitors. Time has a funny way of collapsing when you go back to a place you once loved. You find yourself thinking, I was kissed in that building, I climbed up that tree. This place hasn't changed so terribly much, and so by an extension of logic I must not have changed much, either.

But I have.

That's why I'm the graduation speaker. Think of me as Darwin sailing home on the *Beagle*. I went forth in the world just the way you are about to go forth, and I gathered up all the wondrous things I've seen; now I've brought them back to you. As the graduation speaker I'm the one with the wisdom, or at least that's the assumption, but you as the graduates have something even better: you have youth, which, especially when you multiply it by several hundred, is a thing so fulgent it all but knocks the breath out of those of us who are up on the stage. I'd like to tell you to appreciate your youth, to stop and admire your own health and intelligence, but every writer has a cliché quota and I used up mine by saying, When I was sitting where you are now.

? ? ? ? ? ? ? ? ? ?

When you leave this place, as you will in a couple of hours, be sure to come back. Coming back is the thing that enables you to see how all the dots in your life are connected, how one decision leads you to another, how one twist of fate, good or bad, brings you to a door that later takes you to another door, which, aided by several detours—long hallways and unforeseen stairwells—eventually puts you in the place you are now. Every choice lays down a trail of bread crumbs, so that when you look behind you there appears to be a very clear path that points straight to the place where you now stand. But when you look ahead there isn't a bread crumb in sight—there are just a few shrubs, a bunch of trees, a handful of skittish woodland creatures. You glance from left to right and find no indication of which way you're supposed to go. And so you stand there, sniffing at the wind, looking for directional clues in the growth patterns of moss, and you think, What now?

? ? ? ? ? ? ? ? ? ?

The first time I reached that particular impasse in my life I was in high school, and the burning question concerning my future was where I was going to college. Every day I stood at the window watching for the mailman, and as soon as he had driven safely away (for some reason I thought it was important to conceal my eagerness from the mailman) I would dart out to the box and search for the documents that would determine my fate amongst the grocery store coupons, utility bills, and promotional fliers. But not a single envelope bore my name. It seemed in those days the world only had one question for me, and it was not, How are you feeling? or What is the state of your soul? or What is it you want from life? No, the only thing anyone asked me back then was, Where are you going to college? Everywhere I went I felt as if I were being hounded by my own Greek chorus, and even though all those people hounding me quite possibly had good intentions and were genuinely interested in my future, after a while the questions started to feel like nothing more than a relentless interrogation: a dark room, a single chair, a blinding light in my eyes. "I don't KNOW!" I wanted to scream. "I don't KNOW where I'm going to college!" What if I didn't get accepted any-where? Didn't they ever think about that? What if I had to live at home forever and find a job waiting tables and never got the educa-tion I needed to be a writer? If the people who questioned me had any notion of the depth and the darkness of my fears, I doubt they would have had the temerity to ask me anything at all.

But thanks to the natural order of the universe, for better or for worse, everything eventually changes. One beautiful afternoon the mailman drove off and I ran out to the box and there it was, my entire future in one slim envelope. I ripped into it right there on the lawn and read the contents again and again until I had it committed to memory. I was going to college. In that instant everything in my world was different because I had an answer for the inevitable question. In a funny way that was even more meaningful than the acceptance itself. When the aunt and the dentist and the best friend's mother asked me where I was going, I could reply with a level of nonchalance that made it seem there was never any doubt, "College? Why, I'm going to Sarah Lawrence."

? ? ? ? ? ? ? ? ? ?

Oh, I was set. My sense of time was so underdeveloped that four years sounded like a glorious eternity. I had gotten into the school that I wanted to go to and I would stay there and never have to worry about the future again. Finally I arrived on campus and lugged my suitcases up the stairs of the dreamy little house that was my dorm, put my toothbrush in my assigned toothbrush slot, and unpacked. I knew I wanted to be a writer and so I thought it best to make myself well-rounded, since that's what a writer had to be. I flipped through the course catalog and tried to choose between marine biology and comparative religion and printmaking and economics and Shakespeare. There were so many possibilities that I felt dizzy—what if I picked the wrong one? What if I missed out on the thing I needed the most just because I didn't know I needed it? Back then I thought that a person's education was defined by majors and minors, and that classes set down a map that would guide the rest of my life. If I took the wrong turn now would I feel the repercussions twenty years down the road? How in the world was I qualified to make the decisions that would shape my future? I had thought so much about getting into college that I didn't ever stop to consider what college might be like. All I wanted was to be able to hand the catalog over to my mother and ask her, What now?

? ? ? ? ? ? ? ? ? ?

I was seventeen and a long way from home, having come to New York from Tennessee. There is no way to overstate the fact that all I was in those days was terribly, terribly lonely. I don't even know if that particular brand of loneliness exists anymore, though I suspect that new kinds have sprung up to take its place. There was no e-mail, and in those happy, bygone days only doctors and drug dealers carried cell phones. There was a pay phone downstairs, but it was prohibitively expensive, and anyway, there was always somebody parked on it, usually the beautiful girl from Caracas. We called her the Venezuelan Princess, and she had enough money to talk to her family in South America for hours on end. I went back upstairs with my little sack of quarters and wrote as many letters as I had stamps. I wrote to my parents, my grandmother, and sister. I wrote to all my far-flung girlfriends from high school, but the letters couldn't get to their destinations fast enough for my sadness to be heard. Ultimately this exercise proved as instructive to me as any writing class, since this is where I learned how to transfer the contents of my heart onto a piece of paper. Each letter expressed a different aspect of my circumstances, as each was tailored to its particular

reader, but none of them made me feel any better. Writing is good for many things, but curing loneliness isn't one of them. From my room I heard the voices of the other freshmen who laughed and talked as if they had all been inseparable since Montessori. There was a river full of life rushing right past my door and I didn't have a single clue about how I might jump in.

? ? ? ? ? ? ? ? ? ?

In the end I did the only thing I knew how to do, the thing they always taught us to do in Catholic school: I did unto others. If you want someone to be nice to you, you must be nice to someone else, and since I really knew only one person—my newly assigned adviser Chet Biscardi, who had shown me great kindness in our first meeting—I decided I would bake him a batch of cookies. If it sounds hokey then you can rest assured that's because I was one seriously hokey kid. I walked into town and carried back sacks of flour and sugar and eggs. I bought pans, a measuring cup, a spatula. Because I was on every level starting from scratch those cookies were destined to be the most expensive in history. I mixed up the batter in the little kitchen downstairs in the dorm, beat in the chips and buttered the pans. I set the oven for 350 and waited for it to heat up. I waited. After a suspiciously long time I stuck my hand in and then, feeling a chill, touched the racks. Two pans of raw cookie dough neatly arranged into balls wouldn't have been bad eating but they would have made a very poor gift. I sat there for a minute feeling hopeless, but then decided I couldn't, since the cookies were meant to cure my hopelessness. I picked up the sheets, fixed the bowl of extra dough beneath one arm, and went outside. Next door was another dorm with no doubt equally pathetic appliances, but across the street was a fine-looking house. I don't think it would be an overstatement to say it was a mansion. It was the kind of house one could be certain would have, at the very minimum, one working oven. I was a shy person, but at that moment I was on the edge. I needed a heating element. And so I marched ahead and, using one corner of a pan, knocked on the door.

? ? ? ? ? ? ? ? ?

Alice Ilchman often told this story herself, how during her first week as the new president, still waist-deep in boxes and settling into her house, she opened her front door to find a freshman holding two trays of unbaked cookies. She paused for a minute, wondering if this was some sort of tradition about which no one had informed her, and then she led me back to the kitchen and told me to make myself at home, the most beautiful words that anyone had spoken to me for days. In the time it took the cookies to bake and cool, I met her children and played with her dog. And maybe because I wrote a thank-you note on a paper towel and left it on the table with some cookies, I was invited back to babysit for Alice's daughter, Sarah, and since I proved to be a reliable babysitter, I was also asked back to serve at dinner parties, and then to cook at dinner parties. After all, I clearly knew how to cook.

Had I been the most cunning fresh-man in the history of higher education, I doubt I could have come up with a plan that would have gotten me the very thing I longed for, which was less an oven and more a family to take me in. I never would have had the words to ask for something as large as that. Sometimes the circumstances at hand force us to be braver than we actually are, and so we knock on doors and ask for assistance. Sometimes not having any idea where we're going works out better than we could possibly have imagined.

? ? ? ? ? ? ? ? ? ?

And sometimes, we don't realize what we've learned until we've already known it for a very long time. As much as I came to love

Alice and her daughter and their dog, I loved that house. On the nights that I was babysitting, I would wait until Sarah fell asleep and then I would study the paintings in halls, the leaded glass windows, the heavy sweeping staircase that poured into the foyer, the slender servants' staircase that climbed straight up from the kitchen. I spent a lot of time in the china closet because up until I was invited into that house I never knew such a thing existed—a dozen different sets of china in multiples of twelve, every cup hanging from a tiny gold hook. It was fifteen years later that I needed a mansion in which to stage a hostage takeover in a South American country, that I needed a grand piano and two staircases and, most importantly, a china closet for the characters of my novel to conduct their secret trysts, and thanks to a broken oven, I had it all there, filed away in my memory.

? ? ? ? ? ? ? ? ? ?

It was for me the start of a lesson that I never stop having to learn: to pay attention to the things I'll probably never need to know, to listen carefully to the people who look as if they have nothing to teach me, to see school as something that goes on everywhere, all the time, not just in libraries but in parking lots, in airports, in trees. One of the greatest lessons of my college education came in my junior year when I was lost in Chicago's O'Hare airport. The airports of today bear no resemblance to the airports of twenty years ago, even the ones that are still in the same buildings. I think it would be almost impossible to get lost in an airport now, since you aren't allowed to go into any area for which you are not specifically ticketed. There was a time when people not only walked their loved ones to the gate but walked them onto the plane and sat beside them until it was time to take off. It was not uncommon for people to wander onto the wrong flights and fly to the wrong cities because no one was very diligent about checking tickets. I can remember many times when the flight attendant would close up the door to the plane and say, "We're going to Dallas" and someone would pop up from their seat and say, "What do you mean, Dallas?" Of course, this was not what had happened to me. I had gotten lost long before I ever made it to a plane. I was still trying to find the right terminal. I walked back and forth with my heavy bag, sure I was going to be late. I looked at my ticket. I looked at the signs. I walked back and forth some more. Finally, a young man came up to me and asked the question that anyone who was watching would have known the answer to. "Are you lost?"

? ? ? ? ? ? ? ? ?

He was handsome, with straight, streaky blond hair and a tan. He was maybe five years older than my twenty-year-old self. He had a handful of brochures, a nice smile. I told him I was probably only misplaced.

He looked at my ticket and confirmed that I was a long way away from where I needed to be. "I know the airport," he said. "I'll take you there."

"But then you'll be late for your flight." I was sorry to point this out, seeing as how I was not the kind of girl who was walked to gates by handsome young men. The pleasure and the novelty of the experience were something I'd be sorry to miss.

? ? ? ? ? ? ? ? ?

He shook his head and took my shoulder bag. "What's in here?" he said, sagging beneath its weight. "Lead?"

"Actually, it's zinc." I had brought home several zinc plates to etch for my printmaking class and I was regretting having chosen quite so many. I asked him if he worked at the airport. He didn't look like a guy who worked in the airport. He had on jeans and deck shoes and a dark pink shirt with the sleeves rolled back. He told me he worked there after a fashion: he was a Hare Krishna.

I stopped. Instantly, my good manners fell into combat with my paralyzing fear, fear and manners being two things I had been overburdened with in Catholic school. How did one speak to a Hare Krishna? What did

one say? "Thanks anyway," I said in a weak voice. "I can find it."

"Find what?"

"The gate. I remember where it is now." Hare Krishnas very likely kidnapped girls like me. They brainwashed them into playing tambourines in public parks, made them dance in circles and chant repetitive songs. Thinking of this now it breaks my heart: once the most dangerous person at an airport was a lone Hare Krishna, trying to convert the world to the ways of love and vegetarianism, or that joining a religious sect meant you might have to play an undignified instrument like the tambourine.

He sighed and went on ahead. "Don't be silly."

I felt myself grow pale. He had my suitcase. I looked around at the bustling throng and thought of how there was always safety in numbers. I would walk along with him a ways, not too close, and then I would make my escape. If I lost the bag, so be it. It was not a high price to pay.

"So now you're not talking," he said as we walked on and on. O'Hare is a huge airport and our destination seemed to be somewhere in Southern Illinois. "You don't talk to Hare Krishnas?"

"It's not that," I said, but I couldn't say exactly what it was. The truth is the opportunity to talk to a Hare Krishna had never presented itself to me. A few gates later I tried a more honest tack. "I thought you wore robes."

"We do. But nobody talks to you when you wear the robes." He stopped for a minute to readjust the bag full of my zinc plates, which was digging into his shoulder. "All I want to do is talk to people."

? ? ? ? ? ? ? ? ? ?

Of course he could have been trying to trick me, but if he wasn't I had to admit the right to talk didn't seem like so much to ask, and so I made a decision that was against my cautious nature. I decided to listen. I was lost, after all, and the Hare Krishna had found me. The least I could do was hear him out. When we finally reached the gate I discovered my plane was running two hours late, and so I listened for two hours while he told me what it was like to love God, to love God so much that you would gladly devote every minute of your life to Him, to be so moved by the enormity of His love and

goodness and grace that you wanted to tell other people about this wonderful thing you'd found so they could know it too. "Can you imagine what it's like," he said, "wanting to talk to a woman about love and having her scream at you to get away, or trying to talk to a man about God and having him bury his face in a *Time* magazine? It gets depressing after a while."

"I would think so," I said. It occurred to me that the Hare Krishna had probably been chosen for airport duty because without the robes he fit in so nicely. He had a soft voice and a pleasant manner. He had no doubt been voted the least likely to scare anyone away by his Hare Krishna class and still he failed at his task. But what all the people who had run from him would never know was that he was good company. We ate the chocolate-covered almonds I had in my bag and we talked about God. It was the longest conversation I'd had on the subject since I'd graduated from Catholic school, and I can't imagine it did me any harm. When my plane was finally ready to depart he gave me one of his pamphlets on being a vegetarian and shook my hand. He was a nice man, neither frightening nor mysterious; in fact, I would bet we had more in common than not. The difference was he had answered his own What now. Maybe not forever, but at least for a while.

? ? ? ? ? ? ? ? ? ?

The Hare Krishna didn't convert me (though honestly, I don't believe he had tried) but he did teach me something I should have known all along: people need to talk, and often a willingness to sit and listen is the greatest kindness one person can offer to another. One of the first lessons of child-hood is to be wary of strangers, and while this is good counsel to guard against the world's very small nefarious element, it also teaches us to block out the large majority of those who just have something on their mind they'd like to say. We are taught to be suspi-cious, especially of anyone who might not look like us or share our beliefs. By the time we reach adulthood, many have perfected the art of isolation, of being careful, of not listening in the name of safety. But the truth is that we need to hear other people, all people, especially in those moments when we don't know exactly where we're going ourselves. When it comes to finding our way

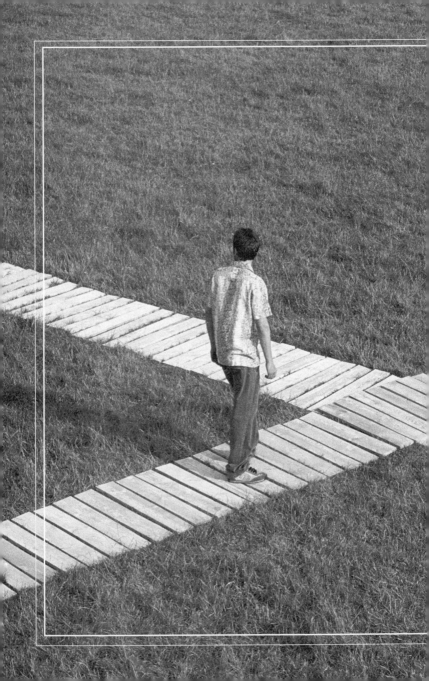

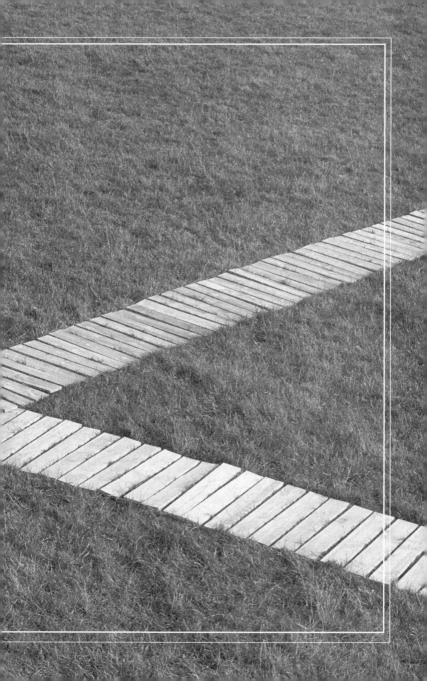

we're better off taking in as much information from as many sources as possible. If
someone told you he didn't need to listen to
other people anymore because frankly he had
life all figured out, he had all the answers,
every single one of them, and was crystal
clear on every last question in the universe,
what could you do with that person but shake
your head in despair? Chances are, anyone
who claims not to need the input of any other
person on the planet is probably crazy. So if
you were sure you didn't have all the answers
and were spending long afternoons asking
yourself What now? wouldn't it be even cra-
zier not to listen to people or to make up your
mind against them based on the most super-
ficial bit of information, say a saffron robe,
perhaps? For the most part wisdom comes
in chips rather than blocks. You have to be

willing to gather them constantly, and from sources you never imagined to be probable. No one chip gives you the answer for everything. No one chip stays in the same place throughout your entire life. The secret is to keep adding voices, adding ideas, and moving things around as you put together your life. If you're lucky, putting together your life is a process that will last through every single day you're alive.

? ? ? ? ? ? ? ? ?

There aren't any Hare Krishnas left in the airports now, or if there are they're flying home to see their parents like the rest of us, but that doesn't mean there is any paucity of people who could use a little attention. Once you decide that strangers are more than just dangerous accidents waiting to happen, you will find yourself able to listen. How much sadness could be averted by taking the time to notice all the people we have come to ignore? Would we in fact be safer and not more at risk if we asked someone to voice his feelings rather than wait until he looked for other means of making himself heard? The world may be telling you to go forward, to climb and to strive and to move briskly ahead, but while you're doing all that, be sure to keep your ears open. Divest yourself of prejudice whenever possible. The Hare Krishna may just be the one who sees you to your gate.

? ? ? ? ? ? ? ? ? ?

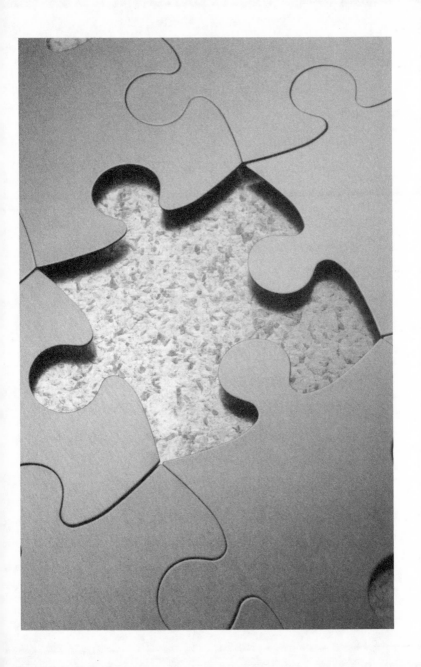

This is the moment when you might be wondering if a novelist is really your best source of practical advice. After all, novelists make things up for a living. We're never going to cure anything. We're not going to get the treaties signed. But novelists are geniuses when it comes to looking at trees. We're very good at staying still and seeing what comes next. People like to tell me I have a glamorous life, and maybe it's true. I was once the answer on *Jeopardy*! (The very hardest answer in the bottom box, and no one knew the question: Who is Ann Patchett?) But I would say that my yearly intake of glamour averages out to be about one hour per month, and that includes giving speeches. Now that's not bad; lots of people don't get anywhere close to an hour a month. But as for the rest of my time, the activity I'm most likely to be engaged in is staring. If staring ever becomes an Olympic event I'll be bringing home the gold. While other people go to work, I stare out the window. I stare at my dog. I stare at blank pieces of paper and paragraphs and

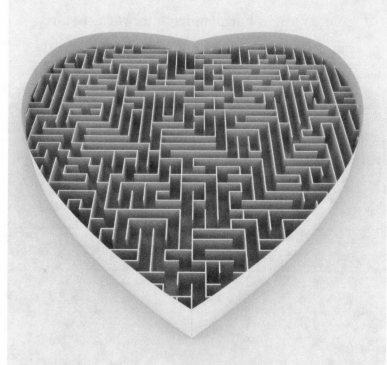

single sentences and a buzzing computer screen. Hours and hours of my day are spent with my eyes glazed over, thinking, waiting, trying to figure things out. The muse is a sweet idea, like the tooth fairy. The muse supposedly comes down like lighting and fills your fingers with the necessary voltage to type up something brilliant. But nobody ever made a living depending on a muse. The rest of us have to go out and find our inspiration, write and rewrite, stare and stare and stare until we know which way to turn. I dated my husband for eleven years before I married him. It was the staring that made me so hesitant.

I just couldn't imagine living in a house with another person when so much of my life was spent sprawled across the sofa, eyes wide open, saying nothing at all.

? ? ? ? ? ? ? ? ? ?

Nothing at all is very much out of fashion these days, as are stillness, silence, and studied consideration. Studied consideration is hard to come by with those little iPod buds stuffed in your ears and the cell phone competing with the Internet. Perhaps we avoid the quiet because we're afraid that the answer to What now? will turn out to be I don't know. Child that I was, I thought admission to college had enabled me to wash my hands of uncertainty. Then, during the second semester of my junior year, some insensitive fool struck the first drumbeat that later rose to a deafening tattoo: What are you going to do after college? they wanted to know. What now? What now? What now?

? ? ? ? ? ? ? ? ? ?

Did they mean, What now as in, What job will you apply for? What exactly are you qualified to do? When I graduated I knew I wanted to be a novelist, but where was the ad in the paper for that one? "Novelist wanted: should be able to stare. Light typing required." What test could I take that would prove I had completed the necessary course-work? What internship would give me a leg up to be a more successful writer? It wasn't just that I couldn't find the key to the door, I couldn't find the door. I batted around like a shuttlecock after graduation, and when I had exhausted my limited resources I moved home to Tennessee and got a job as a line cook. Oddly enough it turned out to be the

one thing for which I had solid qualifications. The very cookies that had gotten me in the front door of the president's house had led to four years of cooking and serving, and when I lost my way that was the direction in which I turned. I had an idea that it was all for the best; I should be doing manual labor, listening to people's stories in a busy restaurant kitchen and then at night having my head free to write them down. I wanted to be a writer of the people. With practice and patience I had become a decent listener, and now I wanted to speak for the common man. It might have been a good idea except for the fact that I could never stay awake once I got home. Being on one's feet all day hauling around boiling kettles of soup, chopping vegetables, making fifteen lunches simultaneously, is exactly why common men work so

hard to make sure their children can get a
college education.

? ? ? ? ? ? ? ? ?

Then one day I burned myself while I
was cleaning out the steam table, and the
owner of the restaurant fired me for my own
safety. I had in essence been told I was unfit
to do the one thing I thought I knew how to
do, and in that moment I realized I would
have to apply to graduate school after all,
even though I had previously believed that
graduate school was nothing but a big stall.
As quickly as the decision had been made,
I discovered that everyone I knew was
suddenly interested in my future again.
Where was I going to go to school? What
would I study? When would I move? It was a

wonderful day when I got my acceptance let-ter from the University of Iowa. I could finally answer their questions again. "Oh," I said. "I've decided to get an M.F.A."

? ? ? ? ? ? ? ? ? ?

Of course you see where this is going. Two years of graduate school shot by in about twenty minutes, and when I wandered out I was just as lost as I had been coming in. No one wasted a second before starting to ask the question again. Apparently there is no statute of limitations on grilling someone about the future. Those of you who have already been accepted to medical school, to law school, to the Peace Corps, stay with me here. I know you think this doesn't apply to you, but it does, because at some point people are going

to want to know where you're going to do your residency or if you've made law review or what you plan on doing upon leaving that village in Uganda. As quickly as you think that everything is set, it all becomes unglued again. A huge part of this is simply luck, the element of life both good and bad that is beyond our control. Sickness comes into the picture of perfect health, true loves catches your eye just as you were setting your foot on the train that would have taken you away forever. Babies are born, jobs are lost, fortunes are made. Wars and suffering pull us backwards while science gives us a second chance we never thought possible. Even if you have it all together you can't know where you're going to end up. There are too many forces, as deep and invisible as tides, that keep us bouncing into places where we never thought we'd wind up. Sometimes the best we can hope for is to be graceful and brave in the face of all of the changes that will surely come. It also helps to have a sense of humor about your own fate, to not think that you alone are blessed when good fortune comes your way, or cursed when it passes you by. It helps if you can realize that this part of life when you don't know what's coming next is often the part that people look back on with the greatest affection. In truth, the moment at which life really does become locked down, most of us are overcome by the desire to break it all apart again so that we can reexperience the variables of youth. As for me, I managed to land a job teaching fiction for one year at a little college in Pennsylvania, and when that was over I wound up back in Nashville working as a waitress at a T.G.I. Friday's. I moved into the guest room in my mother's house. It was exactly the place I had pictured myself going had I never gotten into college at all. Soon after I started working, the district manager came from Memphis to present me with a tiny gold-toned pin in front of the entire assembled waitstaff. WOW, it said. I was the first waitress to score a perfect 100 on her waitressing exam. My six years of higher education had finally paid off. I served fajitas and rolled silverware into napkins and married bottles of ketchup, a delicate procedure in which bottle A must be held on top of bottle B until bottle B is full again. It wasn't a good sign that I demonstrated such adeptness at the transference of ketchup that my superiors thought to praise me for it. The whole time I dreamed of the novels I would write while I heard the Greek chorus singing in my head, What now?

Then one day, while serving strawberry daiquiris to businessmen at four in the afternoon, I had my answer: now you are a waitress with a graduate degree.

? ? ? ? ? ? ? ? ? ?

Receiving an education is a little bit like a garden snake swallowing a chicken egg: it's in you but it takes awhile to digest. I had come to college from twelve years of Catholic girls' school. At the time I thought that mine was the most ridiculous, antiquated secondary education in history. We marched in lines and met the meticulous regulations of the uniform code with cheerful submission. We

bowed and kneeled and prayed. I held open doors and learned how to write a sincere thank-you note and when I was asked to go and fetch a cup of coffee from the kitchen for one of the nuns I fairly blushed at the honor of being chosen. I learned modesty, humility, and how to make a decent white sauce. The white sauce I probably could have done without, but it turns out that modesty and humility mean a lot when you're down on your luck. They went a long way in helping me be a waitress when what I wanted to be was a writer. It turns out those early years of my education which had seemed to me such a waste of time had given me a nearly magical ability to disappear into a crowd. This was not the kind of thing one learned at Sarah Lawrence or the Iowa Writers' Workshop, places that told everyone who came through the door just how special they are. I'm not knocking being special, it was nice to hear, but when it was clear that I was just like everybody else, I was glad to have had some experience with anonymity to fall back on. The nuns were not much on extolling the virtues of leadership. In fact, we were taught to follow. When told to line up at the door, the person who got there first was inevitably pulled from her spot and sent to the back and the person from the back was sent up front to take her place. The idea was that we should not accidentally wind up with too grand an opinion of ourselves, and frankly I regard this as sound counsel. In a world that is flooded with children's leadership camps and grown-up leadership seminars and bestselling books on leadership, I

count myself as fortunate to have been taught a thing or two about following. Like leading, it is a skill, and unlike leading, it's one that you'll actually get to use on a daily basis. It is senseless to think that at every moment of our lives we should all be the team captain, the class president, the general, the CEO, and yet so often this is what we're being prepared for. No matter how many great ideas you might have about salad preparation or the reorganization of time cards, waitressing is not a leadership position. You're busy and so you ask somebody else to bring the water to table four. Someone else is busy and so you clear the dirty plates from table twelve. You learn to be helpful and you learn to ask for help. It turns out that most positions in life, even the big ones, aren't really so much about leadership. Being successful, and certainly being happy, comes from honing your skills in working with other people. For the most part we travel in groups—you're ahead of somebody for a while, then somebody's ahead of you, a lot of people are beside you all the way. It's what the nuns had always taught us: sing together, eat together, pray together.

It wasn't until I found myself relying on my fellow waitress Regina to heat up my fudge sauce for me that I knew enough to be grateful not only for the help she was giving me but for the education that had prepared me to accept it.

? ? ? ? ? ? ? ? ? ?

Is it possible that at the moment in my life when I should have been processing what I had learned in graduate school, I was just

beginning to untangle the lessons of seventh grade? I had studied at the Iowa Writers' Workshop, after all. I had studied writing at Sarah Lawrence with the likes of Allan Gurganus and Grace Paley and Russell Banks. But with all the important books I'd read and all the essential things I had learned about how to write, I didn't become a writer until I worked at Friday's. More specifically, I didn't learn what I really needed to know until the police came late one afternoon and took away the guy who worked the dishwash station. It turns out that I was the only waitress who was willing to wash dishes, and it was while I washed that I finally learned to stare. Oh, maybe I'd played around with staring in school. Maybe I looked out the window every now and then when I was stuck trying to fin-ish a paper, but I had never stared deeply.

Catholic school and college and graduate school had prepared me both for how to be part of a group and how to be the group's leader, but none of them had taught me the most important thing: how to be alone. I had never stared as a way of solving a problem or really seeing the details that make up a story, which is to say I had never just stayed still, been quiet, and thought things through. In the end it was the staring that got me the novelist job I wanted.

? ? ? ? ? ? ? ? ?

As I scrubbed the soup pots and margarita pitchers, I figured out that What now is always going to be a work in progress. What now was never what you think it's going to be, and that's what every writer has to learn. I

had benefitted enormously from my education, from the rigors of class work and the discipline of study, but really, I had learned how to write from the nuns who taught me patience, and from the Hare Krishna who taught me how to devote my entire self to my beliefs even when it meant looking like a fool. I learned from writing letters, but also from Alice Ilchman's openness to a stranger. I learned as much from waitressing as I did from teaching. I learned the most from sticking with my dream even when all signs told me it was time to let go. I came to understand that fiction writing is like duck hunting. You go to the right place at the right time with the right dog. You get into the water before dawn, wearing a little protective gear, then you stand behind some reeds and wait for the story to present itself. This is not to say you are passive. You choose the place and the day. You pick the gun and the dog. You have the desire to blow the duck apart for reasons that are entirely your own. But you have to be willing to accept not what you wanted to have happen, but what happens. You have to write the story you find in the circumstances you've created, because more often than not the ducks don't show up. The hunters in the next blind begin to argue, and you realize they're in love. You see a snake swimming in your direction. Your dog begins to shiver and whine, and you start to think about this gun that belonged to your father. By the time you get out of the marsh you will have written a novel so devoid of ducks it will shock you.

? ? ? ? ? ? ? ? ? ?

I hadn't planned on winding up as a waitress, but the truth is there was a lot about the job I liked even if I didn't think I'd do it forever. I spent my days with good people who were hardworking and resilient. They took their tough times in stride and managed to dream big dreams in between the salads and desserts. I laughed an awful lot in those days, and I felt proud of the money I folded into my pocket at night. Just because things hadn't gone the way I had planned didn't necessarily mean they had gone wrong. It took me a long time of pulling racks of scorching hot glasses out of the dishwasher, the clouds of steam smoothing everything around me into a perfect field of gray, to understand that writing a novel and living a life are very much the same thing. The secret is finding the balance between going out to get what you want and being open to the thing that actually winds up coming your way. What now is not just a panic-stricken question tossed out into a dark unknown. What now can also be our joy. It is a declaration of possibility, of promise, of chance. It acknowledges that our future is open, that we may well do more than anyone expected of us, that at every point in our development we are still striving to grow. There's a time in our lives when we all crave the answers. It seems terrifying not to know what's coming next. But there is another time, a better time, when we see our lives as a series of choices, and What now represents our excitement and our future, the very vitality of life. It's up to you to choose a life that will keep expanding. It takes discipline to remain curious; it takes work to be open to the world—but oh my friends, what noble and glorious work it is. Maybe this is the moment you shift from seeing What now as one more thing to check off the list and start to see it as two words worth living by. This is the day you leave this campus, but if you keep your heart and mind open and are willing to see all of the possibilities that are available to you, it will only be the start of your education.

? ? ? ? ? ? ? ? ? ?

If you're trying to find out what's coming next, turn off everything you own that has an OFF switch and listen. Make up some plans and change them. Identify your heart's truest desire and don't change that for anything. Be proud of yourself for the work you've done.

Be grateful to all the people who helped you do it. Write to them and let them know how you are. You are, every one of you, someone's favorite unfolding story. We will all be anxious to see what happens next.

! ! ! ! ! ! ! ! ! !

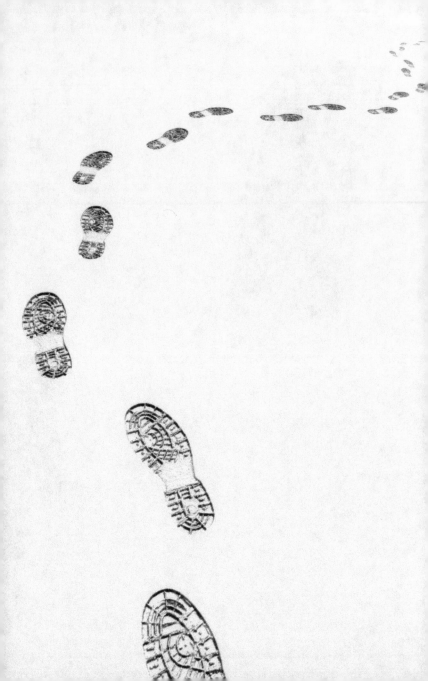

POSTSCRIPT

None of us ever outgrows the need for a teacher. It is a fact I recently rediscovered when I was asked to give this commencement address. I was flattered by the invitation and I worked very hard on my speech. What I came up with in the end was something I deemed to be both serious and grand. I stuck to the admonishment of Ezra Pound's that had meant so much to me when I was an undergraduate: Make it new. I thought I had done exactly that. My speech was not about me, my time in school, or my experiences of trying to become a writer. My speech was ponderous and impersonal, full of necessary information. Like all medicine, it was slightly bitter going down, but I was sure it

would do this class of graduating seniors a world of good.

In the small cusp of time I had between writing the address and delivering it, I was by chance scheduled to give a talk with my favorite former college professor, Allan Gurganus. Much of what I know about writing is something Allan taught me. I admire him both as a novelist and as a person who knows a thing or two about how to live a fully engaged life. Allan had stepped up to the podium at Sarah Lawrence to give a graduation address many years before me, and when I told him I was going to follow in his footsteps he was pleased. He said he'd like to read what I'd written. I said yes without a moment's hesitation.

It had been many, many years since I had turned a paper in for my teacher's review, but wasn't this the perfect moment? Wouldn't Allan's critique be just the thing to make going back to Sarah Lawrence complete? As soon as I was home again I sent it to him, then settled in to wait for my high marks.

His e-mail reply came quickly. "The bit about your father works," he said. "You might be able to build something around that."

I checked my speech again. The bit about my father was nothing but a passing reference, one lonesome sentence. What about the rest of it?

"No," he said. "Sorry. No."

Walking that careful line between gentle and firm, my favorite teacher was then forced to tell his grown-up student that her commencement speech could not be saved. If

you are curious as to its content I would urge you to use your imagination. You will not come up with anything as lifeless as what I had written. Allan said it should be about me, my time in college, my life as a writer. He said it should be funny. In short, it should be everything it wasn't. This was not a situation that called for a rewrite. It was time to let the whole thing go gentle into that good night.

I sat on my couch for a long time and stared out the window. I had no interest in starting over again, but there are some people whom we grant the role of oracle in our lives and when they speak—rarely, gravely—we are well-advised to listen. When I had written my new speech (a shorter version of this book), I did not send it back to Allan. I didn't need to. After all, I am still a good student. I had done everything he told me.

? ? ? ? ? ? ? ? ? ?

The day of graduation started out overcast and then gave way to white shots of lightning slicing through torrents of rain. I waited in the line with my friend Alice Ilchman. She had retired from the post of president and bought a house with her husband a few blocks from campus. Alice stayed remarkably the same over time, with only a little more gray in her straight blond hair. There was always the feeling when I was near her that I was in the presence of a tremendous energy source, the kind of fire that comes from the perfect balance of intelligence and compassion. For as long as I had known her I had wished that I could bottle up just a quarter cup of her effervescence and take it with me to have in the moments when my own intelligence and compassion failed. Alice had been diagnosed with pancreatic cancer about a month before, and the animation that so distinguished my friend had not diminished as her health had waned. Now we sat together on a low stone wall to conserve our energy before the procession. She brushed aside all inquiries about how she was doing, and so while we waited I told her about Allan and the pages I'd thrown away. She considered this for a while. It was as if she could hear my speech coming in from somewhere in the distance and knew just how bad it had been. "Very sound advice," she told me, and held my hand. "Always listen to Allan."

I had listened to Allan, but I didn't fully understand how perceptive he had been until I was up on the platform with all the speakers who came before me. Every one of them was important, instructive, and serious unto dire. I pictured myself delivering my recently abandoned address, being both dull and pedantic, and that picture was a knife through my heart. Holding my new speech in my hands, I had never been so grateful to anyone as I was at that moment to my teacher, who twenty years later and a thousand miles away was still able to save me from making a fool of myself.

? ? ? ? ? ? ? ? ? ?

The sun returned as soon as the procession was over. At the reception afterward a young woman came up and told me that Alice had gotten tired at the ceremony and

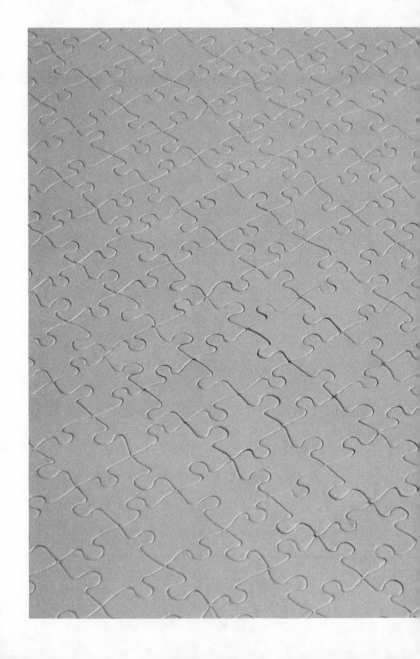

had to go home, but that she wanted me to stop by before I left town. Her daughter, Sarah, now grown up and married, was visiting, and Alice wanted me to say hello. By the time I arrived, Alice had put away her heavy academic gown and hood, and came down the stairs in jeans and a sweater. She was fragile, thin, luminous. When she saw me she held out her arms. "Dear girl," she said, "I knew you'd come."

? ? ? ? ? ? ? ? ? ?

I had never imagined the true gift that would come of being asked to give the commencement address at my college: the chance to say good-bye to my friend.

? ? ? ? ? ? ? ? ? ?

This book lets me pay honor where honor is due. It is a rare and wonderful thing to be able to dedicate a book, to say in print: these are the people I love, the ones to whom I am most grateful.

I do, and I am.

PHOTO CREDITS

HarperCollins books may be purchased for educational, business, or sales promotional use. For information, please write: Special Markets Department, Harper-Collins Publishers, 10 East 53rd Street, New York, NY 10022.

FIRST EDITION

Book design by Chip Kidd

Library of Congress Cataloging-in-Publication Data is available upon request.

ISBN: 978-0-06-134065-9

08 09 10 11 12 QK/RRD 10 9 8 7 6 5 4 3 2 1

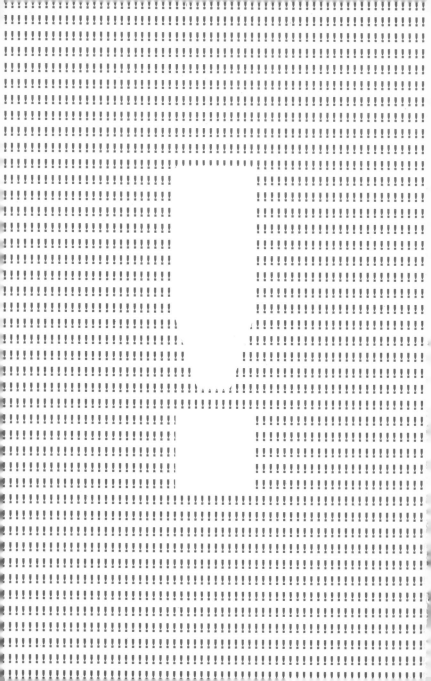